101 Holiday Jokes

Rebecca Magruder

Illustrations by Tom Eaton

SCHOLASTIC INC.
New York Toronto London Auckland Sydney

ISBN 0-590-13282-2

36 9 10 11 12 13 14/0

Printed in the U.S.A. 01
First Scholastic printing, November 1996

What is Count Dracula's favorite time of the year?

The fright before Christmas.

If April showers bring May flowers, what do January blizzards bring?

Lots and lots of snow!

What would you call Frosty the Snowman in May?

A puddle!

Where do reindeer go to dance?

Christmas balls.

What is the army's favorite plant?

Missle toe.

What is a ghoul's favorite holiday song?

The Holly and the Poison Ivy.

If Jewish men light a menorah during Hanukkah, what do Jewish women light?

A womenorah!

Who is reindeer milk best for?

Baby reindeer!

What do pigs sing on New Year's Eve?

Auld Lang Swine.

What do you get a monster for the holidays?

A really big present.

Dora: Who is your favorite ghost from *A Christmas Carol?*
Alonso: The Ghost of Christmas Presents!

When does a reindeer have a trunk?

When it is going on vacation.

How can you tell when Santa Claus is on your roof?

Your television reception is bad!

What's red and shakes like a bowl full of jelly?

Strawberry Jell-O, silly!

If Frosty the Snowman married a vampire, what would they name their child?

Frostbite.

What's the best holiday gift to get for someone who has everything?

Nothing!

What does Frosty the Snowman hang on his Christmas tree?

Icicles.

What's a female sheep's favorite time of the year?

Ewe Near's Eve.

What do you ask a boy skating on thin ice?

"Can you swim?"

Which carol is about small royalty?

Wee Three Kings.

CAROLS YOU HOPE YOU NEVER HEAR!

What carol does every horse love?

Deck the Stalls!

Which carol is about men with beards and moustaches?

God Rest Ye Hairy Gentlemen.

Which carol is about a not-so-smart lad?

The Little Dumber Boy.

Which carol is about an old suit of armor?

Oh Holey Knight.

Which carol is about a mute Lancelot?

Silent Knight.

Which carol is about people who believe in destiny?

Oh Come All Ye Fateful.

Which carol is about a tick and a traveling park service worker?

Away in a Ranger.

Which carol is about a small crazy village?

Oh Little Town of Bedlam.

Which carol is about being confused during the holidays?

The Twelve Daze of Christmas.

Why did Santa cross the road?

To deliver presents.

What's invisible and smells like milk and cookies?

Santa's burps.

What's red and green and appears every Christmas?

An airsick Santa!

What's red, white, and blue and flies in the air?

A frozen Santa!

Who says "Ho, Ho, Ho, Help!"?

Santa falling down your chimney.

Why is Rudolph's nose red?

To match Santa's suit.

What is Kris Kringle's favorite part of a sentence?

A clause.

What is Santa's dog's name?

Santa Paws.

Why does Santa use reindeer to pull his sleigh?

Because moose can't fly, silly!

Who's black and white and says "Ho, Ho, Ho!"?

A penguin in disguise.

Why was Santa angry?

Because of the Grinch Who Stole Christmas!

What do you call Frosty the Snowman's lesser-known brother, the baker?

Frosty the Doughman.

What's the best thing about the holidays?

School vacation!

What's the worst thing about the holidays?

When they're over!

Why does Santa give coal to bad boys and girls?

Oil is too expensive!

What's black and white and red all over?

Santa covered with chimney soot.

What are Santa's favorite girls' names?

Christmas Carol and Candy Cane.

Why doesn't Santa harness horses to his sleigh?

Horses don't have red noses!

Why does Santa have elves in his workshop?

Because the Seven Dwarfs were busy.

Who says "Oh! Oh! Oh!"?

A backwards Santa.

Why did Santa put a clock in his sleigh?

He wanted to see time fly.

What's worse than a grouchy Santa?

A reindeer with a charley horse.

Why is Santa big and jolly?

Because if he were small and mean, he'd be Scrooge!

Why is Santa so jolly?

Wouldn't you be, if you could eat milk and cookies all night long?

What's as big as Santa but weighs nothing at all?

His shadow.

What did Mrs. Claus say about Rudolph?

"Oh, he's such a dear (deer)!"

What does Santa call his Christmas Eve delivery service?

The flight before Christmas.

Which reindeer helps you keep your bathroom clean?

Comet.

What do you get when you cross a menorah with a present?

Eight gifts to unwrap!

What do you get when you cross a toy with a parrot?

A present that talks to itself.

What do you get when you cross a penguin with Rudolph?

A very formally dressed reindeer.

Why is Rudolph's nose so bright?

Because it rhymes with "Won't you guide my sleigh tonight?"

Why was Rudolph chosen to lead the sleigh?

Because he nose better than the other reindeer.

What do you get when you cross Christmas with Hanukkah?

Eight times the fun!

What did the silly girl say about the dreidel top?

"Where's the dreidel bottom?"

Why was Rudolph's nose red?

He was embarrassed!

Why did the silly boy take the Christmas tree to a barber?

Because his mother said it needed to be trimmed.

Why did the silly boy bring a pack of cards to the holiday party?

To deck the halls.

When is a sleigh not a sleigh?

When it's turning into your driveway.

What's worse than Rudolph with a cold?

Frosty the Snowman with a fever!

Why did the silly Jewish boy insult his brother during Hanukkah?

He thought it was the Festival of Slights!

Why do mummies like the holidays?

Because of all the wrapping.

TO MOMMY LOVE MUMMY
MERRY CHRISTMAS
HAPPY HOLIDAYS

What do you get when you cross a mummy with a gift?

A very tightly wrapped present.

What do you get a huge, hairy gorilla for Christmas?

Anything he wants!

What's black and white and red all over?

Santa Penguin.

Why did the silly boy think that every day was Christmas in Hollywood?

Because it's called Tinsel Town.

What's the best thing to give your parents for the holidays?

A list of everything you want!

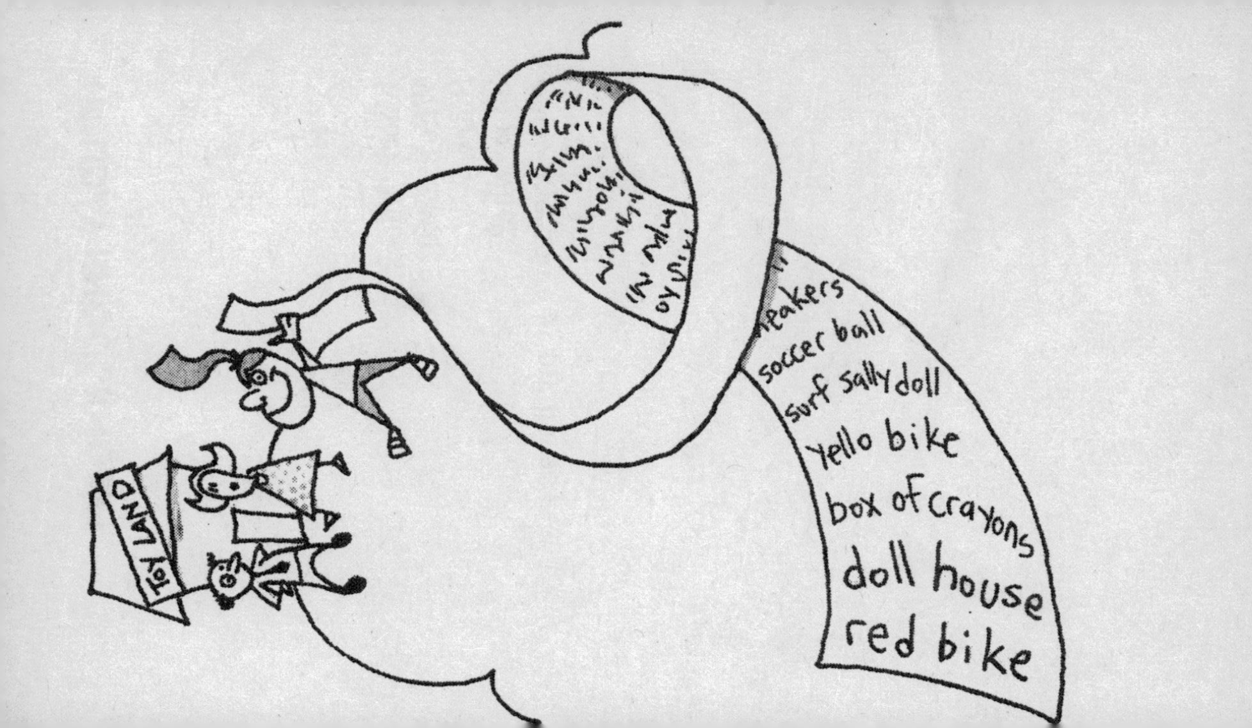
TOY LAND
soccer ball
surf sally doll
yello bike
box of crayons
doll house
red bike

Knock, knock.
Who's there?
Snow.
Snow who?
Snow one home at my house.

Knock, knock.
Who's there?
Sleigh.
Sleigh who?
Sleigh another dragon, Sir Lancelot!

Knock, knock.
Who's there?
Yule.
Yule who?
Yule have fun during the holidays!

Knock, knock.
Who's there?
Stockings.
Stocking who?
Stockings'll keep your feet warm!

What's the best part about being a reindeer?

The frequent flyer miles.

Knock, knock.
Who's there?
Gladys.
Gladys who?
Gladys not me who got coal in my stocking!

Knock, knock.
Who's there?
Orange.
Orange who?
Orange you glad you were good all year?

Knock, knock.
Who's there?
Sara.
Sara who?
Sara monster on the roof or is that Santa Claus?

Knock, knock.
Who's there?
Ice.
Ice who?
Ice wear (I swear) I've been good all year!

Knock, knock.
Who's there?
Gift.
Gift who?
Gift him two presents, now he wants two more!

Knock, knock.
Who's there?
Hope.
Hope who?
Hope you had nice holidays!

REINDEER RIDDLES

Why is Rudolph's nose red?

He has a cold!

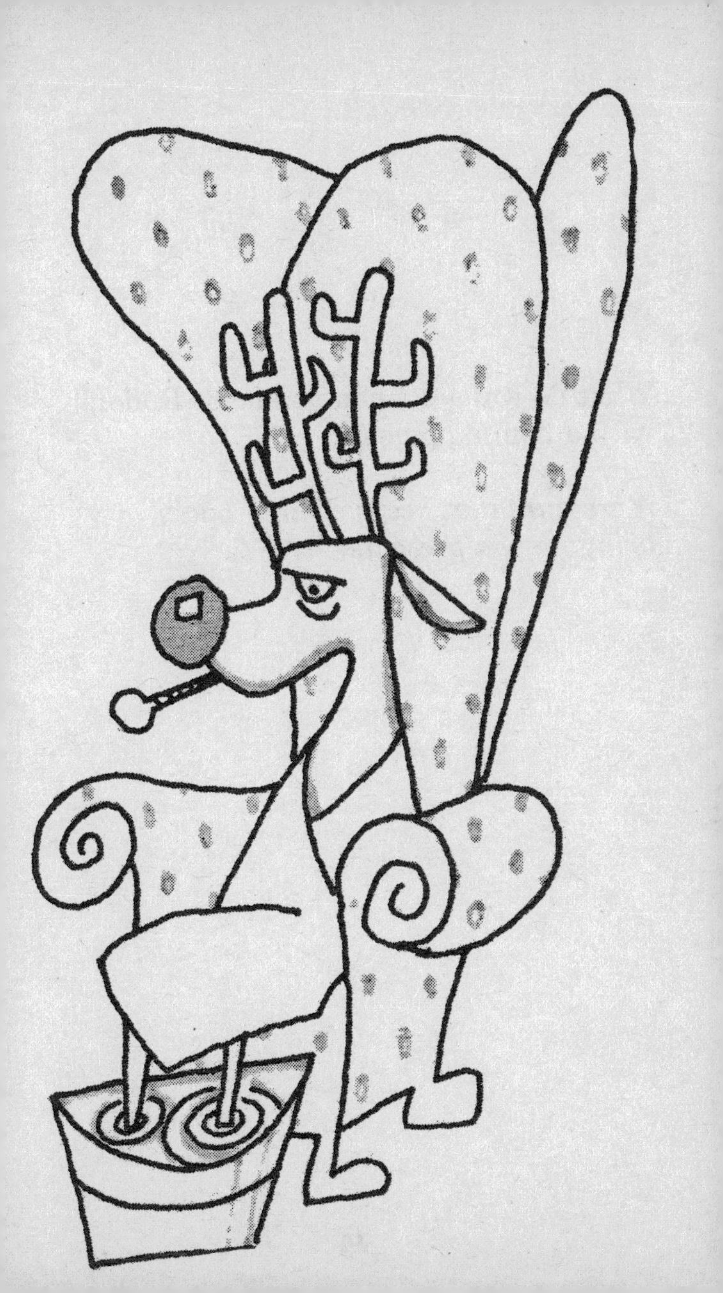

What do you get when you cross Rudolph with a homing pigeon?

A creature that keeps coming back, bringing you presents!

Why is Rudolph's nose red?

Vixen punched him!

Knock, knock.
Who's there?
Elf.
Elf who?
Elf me pick up this heavy present.

What's worse then a hoarse caroller?

A reindeer that's afraid of heights.

What do you get when you cross a toy with an elf?

A present that wraps itself.

Melissa: Why didn't Santa visit your house?
Amy: We don't have a chimney!

Knock, knock.
Who's there?
Oswald.
Oswald who?
Oswald four candy canes and now my stomach hurts!

Knock, knock.
Who's there?
Seymour.
Seymour who?
Seymour Christmas lights this year?

Knock, knock.
Who's there?
Megan.
Megan who?
Megan me will light the menorah tonight.

Knock, knock.
Who's there?
Hugo.
Hugo who?
Hugo to the school holiday show?

Knock, knock.
Who's there?
Gus.
Gus who?
Gus who's coming to dinner!

Why does Santa have a garden?

Because he likes to hoe, hoe, hoe.

David: Why are you bringing that plant to school?
Jonathan: For the holly-days.

SCHOOL
HOLIDAY
PLAY
TONIGHT

Elf: Santa, please slow down. I get nervous when you speed around the corners.
Santa: Do what I do. Close your eyes!

Knock, knock.
Who's there?
Noah.
Noah who?
Noah more holiday jokes, please!